Editor
Amethyst W. Gaidelis, M.A.

Editor in Chief
Ina Massler Levin, M.A.

Creative Director
Karen J. Goldfluss, M.S. Ed.

Cover Artist
Barb Lorseyedi

Imaging
James Edward Grace
Craig Gunnell

CD Application Programmer
Charles Payne

Publisher
Mary D. Smith, M.S. Ed.

Interactive Learning

for All INTERACTIVE WHITEBOARDS

TCR 3611

Paragraph Editing

CORRELATED TO COMMON CORE STANDARDS

Lee wished he could live in the trees like the birds. Lee built himself a tree house. the birds liked Lee's new tree house. They built nests in lee's tree. The sparrows nests is closest to his house.

★ Developed for ALL Interactive Whiteboards
★ 100 ready-to-edit paragraphs to practice and review grammar, punctuation, and spelling
★ Includes Common Core State Standards

Teacher Created Resources

Teacher Created Resources

6421 Industry Way
Westminster, CA 92683
www.teachercreated.com

ISBN: 978-1-4206-3611-6

© 2013 Teacher Created Resources
Made in U.S.A.

Teacher Created Resources

Table of Contents

Introduction

Imagine a classroom tool that could make grammar and spelling exciting and engaging for your students. *Paragraph Editing* is a program that has been designed to do all of this and more. Compatible with all interactive whiteboards, *Paragraph Editing* offers the many advantages of touchscreen technology and allows your students to participate in learning like never before.

Each *Paragraph Editing* CD comes loaded with the paragraphs from this book. The paragraphs are divided into 25 units, with new grammar rules incorporated into each of the first 15 units. In this way, grammar, punctuation, and spelling concepts are introduced and then reinforced in a systematic manner, allowing students to practice each concept before learning new ones. The final 10 units of each book and CD offer a cumulative reinforcement of all of the rules and concepts previously learned.

These paragraphs can be accessed and printed from the CD or copied from the book. They can be done as in-class work or assigned as homework. Corrections to these paragraphs can then be made on individual computers or on an interactive whiteboard in front of the class. All it takes is a finger or a special pen, depending on the interactive board you use. You and your students can correct the sentences in these ways:

☞ by writing and drawing directly onto the interactive whiteboard

☞ by grabbing punctuation stamps built into the program and dragging them over the corresponding errors

An array of buttons and menus allows you to do (and undo) every correction quickly and easily and in six custom colors. Best of all, it takes just one quick click of a button for teachers and students to see the correct answers. And, as an added teaching tool, another touch of a button will show students the locations of the paragraph's errors without revealing the actual answers.

In addition to the paragraphs included on the CD, the *Paragraph Editing* program allows you to create and save thousands of custom paragraphs. The program can even make incorrect versions of your custom creations by adding errors for you. Teachers can use this tool to tap into their class's creativity with student-generated paragraphs and peer-editing exercises.

Common Core State Standards

The activities in this book meet one or more of the following Common Core State Standards. (© Copyright 2010. National Governors Association Center for Best Practices and Council of Chief State School Officers. All rights reserved.) For more information about the Common Core State Standards, go to *http://www.corestandards.org/*.

Reading Standards: Foundational Skills
Phonics and Word Recognition
Standard 3: RF.2.3 Know and apply grade-level phonics and word analysis skills in decoding words. • RF.2.3f: Recognize and read grade-appropriate irregularly spelled words.
Fluency
Standard 4: RF.2.4 Read with sufficient accuracy and fluency to support comprehension. • RF.2.4a: Read grade-level text with purpose and understanding. • RF.2.4c: Use context to confirm or self-correct word recognition and understanding, rereading as necessary.

Language Standards
Conventions of Standard English
Standard 1: L.2.1 Demonstrate command of the conventions of standard English grammar and usage when writing or speaking. • L.2.1b: Form and use frequently occurring irregular plural nouns. • L.2.1d: Form and use the past tense of frequently occurring irregular verbs. • L.2.1f: Produce, expand, and rearrange complete simple and compound sentences. **Standard 2:** L.2.2 Demonstrate command of the conventions of standard English capitalization, punctuation, and spelling when writing. • L.2.2a: Capitalize holidays, product names, and geographic names. • L.2.2c: Use an apostrophe to form contractions and frequently occurring possessives. • L.2.2d: Generalize learned spelling patterns when writing words.
Knowledge of Language
Standard 3: L.2.3 Use knowledge of language and its conventions when writing, speaking, reading, or listening.

About the CD

The real flexibility and interactivity of the *Paragraph Editing* program shine through in the resources included on the CD.

☞ Install the CD

Just pop the CD that accompanies this book into your PC or Mac, and you and your students can begin editing paragraphs at individual computers or on the interactive whiteboard in your classroom.

> **Quick Tip:** Step-by-step installation instructions and some troubleshooting tips are provided in the "Read Me" file on the CD.

☞ The Main Menu

Once you have installed the CD, the Main Menu will appear on your computer screen or interactive whiteboard.

> **Quick Tip:** The Main Menu will open up in full-screen mode. If you wish to resize the Main Menu screen, hit the ESC button. This will allow you to adjust it as needed.

From the Main Menu, you can access all of the features and resources available in the program. To get a detailed explanation of these features, click on the Guide button. This will take you to the *Paragraph Editing* User's Guide.

☞ The User's Guide

Everything you need to know in order to use and operate the *Paragraph Editing* CD and program can be found in the User's Guide. This is also where you will find a useful one-page handout of the editing symbols used in the program. These marks are available as punctuation stamps on the editing screen for each sentence.

Main Menu Screen

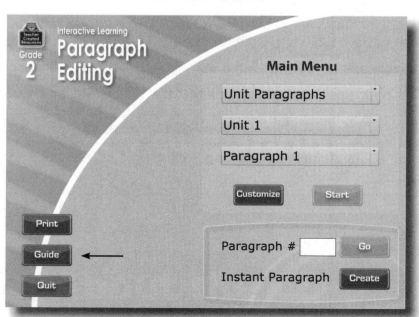

About the CD (cont.)

The User's Guide on the CD contains a lot of important and helpful information. However, you may wish to immediately begin editing paragraphs with your students. The following Quick-Start Guide will help you do just that.

Quick-Start Guide for Editing Paragraphs

1. **Launch the Program:** Load the CD and launch the program. If needed, follow the installation instructions given in the "Read Me" file on the CD.

2. **Click the Start Button:** You can access the **Start** button from the **Main Menu** screen. (See the graphic to the right.) This will take you directly to the editing screen. (See the graphic at the bottom of the page.)

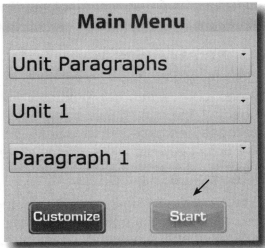

3. **Edit the Paragraph:** Write, draw, or paint directly onto the screen. You may also use the punctuation stamps located on either side of the screen. Grab, drag, and drop these stamps onto, above, or below the word to correct the errors.

4. **Check Your Work:** Click on the **Show Errors** button to give your students hints about where the errors can be found in the paragraph. Click on the **Show Correct** button to reveal the correct version of the paragraph.

5. **Edit a New Paragraph:** Click on the **Next** button to continue the editing lesson with a new paragraph.

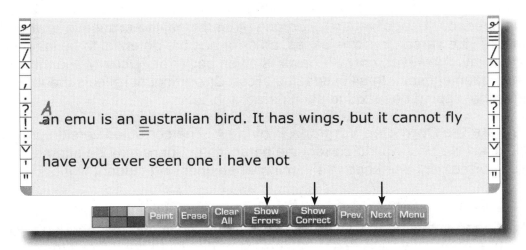

About the Book

There are two main components to the *Paragraph Editing* program: a book and a CD. These two parts were designed to be complementary, but they can also be used independently of one another. This 112-page book contains the following features:

☞ **Common Core State Standards (page 3)**

The grammar rules and concepts reviewed in this book meet Common Core State Standards for grade-level appropriateness.

☞ **Tips for Using the CD (pages 4–5)**

These two pages include tips for getting started with the CD that accompanies this book.

☞ **Grammar Rules (pages 7–11)**

This book includes a list of the punctuation, capitalization, and usage rules students will need to know in order to correct the paragraphs. New rules are introduced in each of the first 15 units, allowing students to learn increasingly difficult grammar concepts at a measured pace, while reviewing the ones they have previously learned. The final 10 units serve as a cumulative review of the rules learned in the first 15 units.

☞ **Ready-To-Be-Edited Paragraphs (pages 12–111)**

On each even-numbered page of this section, there are two error-filled paragraphs. (In all, this book contains a total of 100 unique paragraphs.) These paragraphs contain plenty of space between lines so students may add editing marks and rewrite incorrectly spelled words. Copy these pages for use as in-class assignments or send them home as homework.

On the odd-numbered pages that follow, the corrected versions of the paragraphs are given. The revisions are shown in gray, and a summary of the errors that can be found in each paragraph is provided.

Note About the Summary of Errors: The terms used in this list are meant to help you quickly locate specific types of errors. Many terms refer to both the omission and the misuse of that element. *Examples:* The term "Periods" is given when a period is missing and also when one is used incorrectly (in place of a question mark, for example). "Capitalization" is a broad term used to refer to any instance where a capital or lowercase letter is needed. "Usage" refers to, among other things, the misuse of *a* when *an* is needed, or vice versa. In some cases, an error has the potential to be labeled in more than one way. However, only one label is given per error. Usually, the most specific term has been chosen. In all cases, the "Total Errors" count reflects the total number of changes that should be made to each paragraph.

Note About the Corrected Versions Provided: The corrected version provided shows what is often the best way to correct the paragraph. There may be alternate ways that are also correct. Please keep this in mind when checking student work.

☞ **Editing Marks (page 112)**

The final page of this book contains a full list of the editing marks needed to correct the paragraphs. You may wish to display this list or distribute copies of it to your students.

Grammar Rules

The following pages include most of the grammar, usage, and punctuation rules students will need to know to edit the sentences in this book. The units in which these rules are applicable are listed in parentheses after each rule.

Rule 1: Capitalize the word *I*. **(Units 1–25)**

- **Scott and <u>I</u> are friends.**

Rule 2: A *sentence* is a group of words that tells a complete thought. Capitalize the first word in a sentence. A *statement* is a sentence that tells something. Put a period at the end of a telling sentence. **(Units 1–25)**

- **<u>My</u> dog is black<u>.</u>**

Rule 3: A *question* is a sentence that asks something. Put a question mark at the end of an asking sentence. **(Units 1–25)**

- **Do you have a pet<u>?</u>**

Rule 4: An *exclamation* is a sentence that shows feeling. It ends with an exclamation mark. **(Units 1–25)**

- **We won the game<u>!</u>**

Rule 5: A *command* is a sentence that tells someone to do something. It ends with a period or an exclamation mark. **(Units 1–25)**

- **Please print your name<u>.</u>**
- **Get out of the street<u>!</u>**

Rule 6: *Nouns* are words that name people, places, things, ideas, and animals. **(Units 1–25)**

- **The <u>doctor</u> sat in his <u>office</u>.**
- **<u>Honesty</u> is the best <u>policy</u>.**

Rule 7: *Proper nouns* name specific people, places, things, and ideas, and animals. A proper noun begins with a capital letter. *Common nouns* are not specific. A common noun does not begin with a capital letter. **(Units 1–25)**

- **The <u>dog</u> is named <u>Max</u>.** (common noun = *dog*; proper noun = *Max*)

Rule 8: Capitalize the days of the week, months of the year, and holidays. Do not capitalize seasons of the year. **(Units 2–25)**

- **Is <u>Memorial Day</u> on a <u>Monday</u> in <u>May</u>?**
- **My favorite season is <u>spring</u>.**

Grammar Rules *(cont.)*

Rule 9: An *abbreviation* is a short form of a word. Capitalize name titles and put a period after ones that have been shortened into an abbreviation. Also capitalize and put a period after initials, which are letters used instead of a full name. **(Units 3–25)**

- **The shop is owned by <u>Mr.</u> Payne.**
- **My dentist is <u>Dr.</u> Anna Lee.**
- **The author is <u>J.P.</u> Wilson.**

Rule 10: A *colon* is used between the hour and minutes when writing the time of day. **(Units 4–25)**

- **We went to school at 8<u>:</u>00.**

Rule 11: Use a *comma* to separate the day and year or to separate the day and month. Use a comma to separate a city and state or country. **(Units 5–25)**

- **She was born on Thursday<u>,</u> November 2<u>,</u> 2006.**
- **Andrea flew from Houston<u>,</u> Texas, to Paris<u>,</u> France.**

Rule 12: A *series* is a list of three or more items. Use a comma to separate three or more words or groups of words in a series. **(Units 6–25)**

- **Would you rather have pizza<u>,</u> pasta<u>,</u> or a hamburger?**

Rule 13: A *singular noun* names one person, place, thing, or idea. A *plural noun* names more than one person, place, thing, or idea. Add *s* to most nouns to make them plural. Add *es* to words that end in *s, ch, sh, x,* and *z*. **(Units 7–25)**

- **I have two small <u>dogs</u> and one big <u>dog</u>.**
- **I see one blue <u>dish</u> and two red <u>dishes</u>.**

Rule 14: Use *a* or *an* before singular nouns. Use *a* before words that begin with a consonant sound. Use *an* before words that begin with a vowel or vowel sound. **(Units 7–25)**

- **He ate <u>a</u> piece of toast and <u>an</u> egg <u>an</u> hour before school began.**

Rule 15: Nouns that end in the letter *y* have special rules for making plurals. If the word ends with a vowel followed by *y*, just add *s*. If the word ends with a consonant followed by *y,* change the *y* to *i* and add *es*. **(Units 8–25)**

- **Dad put his <u>keys</u> in his coat pocket.**
- **I went to three birthday <u>parties</u> in June.**

Grammar Rules *(cont.)*

Rule 16: Nouns that end in *f* or *fe* also have a special rule for making plurals. In most words, change the *f* to *v* and add *es*. **(Units 8–25)**

- **I found six butter <u>knives</u> and one bread <u>knife</u> in the drawer.**
- **One <u>calf</u> has black spots. Two <u>calves</u> have brown spots.**

Rule 17: *Irregular plural nouns* are nouns that have a special spelling when they are plural. Memorize the spellings of such irregular plurals as *foot/feet*, *child/children*, *tooth/teeth*, *mouse/mice*, and *fish/fish*. **(Units 8–25)**

- **I brush my <u>teeth</u> twice a day.**
- **The <u>children</u> all loved to see the clown.**

Rule 18: A *possessive noun* shows ownership. Use an *apostrophe* and an *s* (*'s*) after a noun to show that something belongs to one person or thing. To form the plural possessive of a plural noun that ends in *s*, add only an apostrophe. If the plural noun does not end in *s*, add an apostrophe and an *s*. **(Units 9–25)**

- **<u>Beth's</u> guitar is sitting next to <u>Jess's</u> drum set.**
- **Both of his <u>brothers'</u> bikes are blue.**
- **We visited the <u>children's</u> library yesterday.**

Rule 19: A *pronoun* is a word that is used in place of a noun. Use the pronouns *we/us, she/he, her/him,* and *they/them* correctly. Use reflexive pronouns such as *myself, yourself, himself, herself,* and *ourselves* correctly. **(Units 10–25)**

Use *we* when you and others are doing something.

Use *she/he/they* when a person or group that doesn't include you is doing something.

Use *us* when something happens to you and others.

Use *her/him/them* when something is happening to a person or a group that doesn't include you.

Use reflexive pronouns when people are doing things for or to themselves.

- **<u>We</u> went to school.**
- **<u>He</u> is riding the bike.**
- **Sam gave <u>him</u> a ride.**
- **<u>They</u> gave the trophy to <u>us</u>.**
- **<u>She</u> will cook dinner for <u>herself</u>.**
- **Bill took <u>her</u> to the movie.**

Rule 20: Use *I* and *me* correctly. Use the pronoun *I* when you are doing something. Use the pronoun *me* when something happens to you. **(Units 10–25)**

- **Mom and <u>I</u> went to Hawaii.**
- **She waved to Bob and <u>me</u>.**

Grammar Rules *(cont.)*

Rule 21: The *verb* often shows the action of the sentence. When the subject of the sentence is singular, an *s* or *es* is usually added to the verb (except with the pronouns *I* or *you*.) When the subject is plural, an *s* is not added to the verb. **(Units 11–25)**

- **Ryan <u>eats</u> a lot of food. Eric and Bob <u>eat</u> more food.**

- **You <u>eat</u> broccoli for lunch. I do not <u>eat</u> broccoli.**

- **The school <u>fixes</u> lunch for us. They <u>fix</u> lunch for us every day.**

Rule 22: The verbs *am, are, is, was,* and *were* are forms of the word *be.* They are not action words. Instead, they tell what someone or something is like. **(Units 11–25)**

Use *am* with the word *I.*

Use *is* and *are* when talking about what is happening now.

Use *was* and *were* when talking about things that have already happened.

Use *is* and *was* when talking about one person, place, thing, or idea.

Use *are* and *were* when talking about more than one person, place, thing, or idea, and with the word *you.*

- **I <u>am</u> six years old.**
- **You <u>are</u> older than I am.**
- **Jim <u>is</u> seven years old.**

- **Last year, Jim <u>was</u> six.**
- **Kate and Nate <u>are</u> eight.**
- **They <u>were</u> seven last year.**

Rule 23: A *present-tense verb* shows action that happens now. A *past-tense verb* tells about an action that already happened. Add *ed* to most verbs to form the past tense. In addition to *s* and *es*, the ending *ing* can also be added to present-tense verbs. If the verb has a single vowel and ends with a consonant, the last consonant is usually doubled before adding *ed* or *ing*. If the word ends with a silent *e*, drop the final *e* before adding *ed* or *ing*. **(Units 12–25)**

- **The car <u>stops</u> here now. It also <u>stopped</u> here yesterday. Will it be <u>stopping</u> here every day?**

- **I <u>wave</u> goodbye. I <u>waved</u> to everybody. I am <u>waving</u> my hand.**

Rule 24: If a verb ends with a consonant and *y*, change the *y* to *i* and add *es* to form the present-tense verb. If a verb ends with a consonant and *y*, change the *y* to *i* and add *ed* to form a past-tense verb. **(Units 12–25)**

- **Each team <u>tries</u> to win.**
- **I <u>tried</u> to hit a home run.**

Grammar Rules (cont.)

Rule 25: The past tense of some verbs is made by changing the spelling. **(Units 12–25)**

- **Last week my dog <u>ran</u> away.** *(run)*
- **He <u>bought</u> some milk at the store.** *(buy)*
- **He <u>drew</u> a picture in art class.** *(draw)*

Rule 26: A *contraction* is a word made by joining two words. When joining the words, a letter or letters are left out. An apostrophe is put in the word at the spot where the letter or letters are missing. **(Units 13–25)**

- **<u>We are</u> going home.   <u>We're</u> going home.**
- **She <u>did not</u> see him.   She <u>didn't</u> see him.**
- **<u>He will</u> be there soon.   <u>He'll</u> be there soon.**

Rule 27: A name can be made into a contraction as well as a possessive by adding *'s*. The *'s* can mean *is* or *has*, depending on the sentence. **(Units 13–25)**

- **<u>Mary's</u> going to Canada this summer.** *(contraction)*
- **I saw <u>Mary's</u> car parked in the lot.** *(possessive)*

Rule 28: A *homophone* is a word that sounds the same as another word but has a different spelling or meaning. Be careful not to confuse these and other misused words, such as *are/our* and *it's/its.* **(Units 14–25)**

- **I can <u>see</u> the ship out on the <u>sea</u>.**
- **Scott <u>ate</u> <u>eight</u> donuts for breakfast!**
- **<u>Are</u> you coming to <u>our</u> house today?**
- **<u>It's</u> time to give the dog <u>its</u> bath.**

Rule 29: When writing the title of a book, movie, play, newspaper, music collection, or television show, underline the entire title and capitalize the first word, the last word, and each important word. Follow the same capitalization rules but use quotation marks around the titles of stories, poems, and songs. **(Units 15–25)**

- **We read the book <u>Holes</u> in class.**
- **We listened to "Somewhere Over the Rainbow" from <u>The Wizard of Oz</u>.**

the Amazon is a huge river It is in South america. sometimes, there are biig waves in the Amazon the ocean tides cause the big waves.

pow stacie stared as the ball sailed over the pitcher and past the outfield fence. It was her first home run Stacie dropped the bat and ran the bases one by one

the Amazon is a huge river It is in South america. sometimes, there are ~~biig~~ big waves in the Amazon the ocean tides cause the big waves.

Unit 1 • Paragraph 1 Errors

Capitalization 4
Periods 2
Spelling 1

Total Errors: 7

pow stacie stared as the ball sailed over the pitcher and past the outfield fence. It was her first home run Stacie dropped the bat and ran the bases one by one

Unit 1 • Paragraph 2 Errors

Capitalization 2
Exclamation Marks 1
Periods 2

Total Errors: 5

Name: _____ Date: _____

Do you like to be happy Walt disney

did. He liked to make people laugh. walt

loved to draw, and he liked to tak

pictures. Walt went to hollywood

i spied a spider on my desk. As i

tiptoed toward my desk, the spyder began

to move. I screamed and dashed from

the rom

Do you like to be happy Walt disney did. He liked to make people laugh. walt loved to draw, and he liked to tak pictures. Walt went to hollywood

Unit 1 • Paragraph 3 Errors

Capitalization 3
Periods 1
Question Marks . . 1
Spelling 1

Total Errors: 6

i spied a spider on my desk. As i tiptoed toward my desk, the ~~spyder~~ spider began to move. I screamed and dashed from the rom

Unit 1 • Paragraph 4 Errors

Capitalization 2
Periods 1
Spelling 2

Total Errors: 5

it was saturday morning It was the middle of Summer, and it was very hot. Amy and ana made lemonade in a plastic pitcher. They sold the drinks for one quarter each.

Maya is very busy. On monday and Wednesday, maya takes a crafts class On thursday and Saturday, Maya has Soccer practice. Friday night is famly night.

it was saturday morning. It was the middle of Summer, and it was very hot. Amy and ana made lemonade in a plastic pitcher. They sold the drinks for one quarter each.

Unit 2 • Paragraph 5
Errors

Capitalization 4
Periods 1

Total Errors: 5

Maya is very busy. On monday and Wednesday, maya takes a crafts class. On thursday and Saturday, Maya has Soccer practice. Friday night is famly night.

Unit 2 • Paragraph 6
Errors

Capitalization 4
Periods 1
Spelling 1

Total Errors: 6

February is a busy month for holidays.

Groundhog day is in february. It actually

is a day to forecast how much longer

winter will be around After Groundhog

Day, there is valentine's day There is

also president's Day

It was saturday morning, and it was

raining! Kenny moaned and puled the

covers over his hed. just then, he felt a

pounce on his stomach He peeked out,

and there was his cat, buttons

February is a busy month for holidays. Groundhog day is in february. It actually is a day to forecast how much longer winter will be around. After Groundhog Day, there is valentine's day. There is also president's Day.

Unit 2 • Paragraph 7 Errors

Capitalization 5
Periods 3

Total Errors: 8

It was saturday morning, and it was raining! Kenny moaned and puled the covers over his hed. just then, he felt a pounce on his stomach. He peeked out, and there was his cat, buttons.

Unit 2 • Paragraph 8 Errors

Capitalization 3
Periods 2
Spelling 2

Total Errors: 7

How do yoo get bananas from south america They are put on a big ship or plane. When they get to the U S , they are put on a train and then a truck. the bananas end up at your store

In matt's class, there are two students named george. His teacher, ms Dana, calls them George L and George m George L likes to write his initials, G L , on letters he writes to friends.

How do ~~yoo~~ you get bananas from south america? They are put on a big ship or plane. When they get to the U.S., they are put on a train and then a truck. the bananas end up at your store.

Unit 3 • Paragraph 9 Errors

Capitalization 3
Periods........ 3
Question Marks .. 1
Spelling 1

Total Errors: 8

In matt's class, there are two students named george. His teacher, ms. Dana, calls them George L. and George m. George L. likes to write his initials, G. L., on letters he writes to friends.

Unit 3 • Paragraph 10 Errors

Capitalization 4
Periods......... 6

Total Errors: 10

~~~~~~

Bobby middler has a little sister named

tamara jade, but everyone calls her t.j.

In august, the family is going to Disney

world in Orlando, Florida. bobby and T J

can't wate.

~~~~~~

since he was a childe, William had

dreamed of commanding a starship. Now

here hee was, capt W R nichols, about to

take off on the first manned mission to

Mars. He was thrilled

Bobby middler has a little sister named tamara jade, but everyone calls her t.j. In august, the family is going to Disney world in Orlando, Florida. bobby and T. J. can't wait.

Unit 3 • Paragraph 11
Errors

Capitalization 8
Periods 2
Spelling 1

Total Errors: 11

since he was a childe, William had dreamed of commanding a starship. Now here hee was, capt. W. R. nichols, about to take off on the first manned mission to Mars. He was thrilled.

Unit 3 • Paragraph 12
Errors

Capitalization 3
Exclamation Marks 1
Periods 3
Spelling 2

Total Errors: 9

I wake up at 600 each morning and get ready for school i go downstairs and eat breakfast Then I go outside to wait for the bus. Once i arrive at school, I walk with my Friends, charlotte and molly, to the classroom

It was 1000 p.m. and Megan the cow could not slep The moon was much too bright. the Clouds wanted to help Megan They moved carefully in front of the moon. Megan quickly went to sleep

I wake up at 6:00 each morning and get ready for school. I go downstairs and eat breakfast. Then I go outside to wait for the bus. Once I arrive at school, I walk with my friends, Charlotte and Molly, to the classroom.

Unit 4 • Paragraph 13 Errors

Capitalization 5
Colons 1
Periods 3

Total Errors: 9

It was 10:00 p.m. and Megan the cow could not sleep. The moon was much too bright. The Clouds wanted to help Megan. They moved carefully in front of the moon. Megan quickly went to sleep.

Unit 4 • Paragraph 14 Errors

Capitalization 2
Colons 1
Periods 3
Spelling 1

Total Errors: 7

amy did not do her math homework.

right after schol, a friend came over, and

they watched a show. At 430, she baked

an Apple Pie for that night's dessert After

diner, amy was slepy, so she turned out

the light and went to bed early

It is 1230 p.m. It is hot and sunny.

sam is going to play in the pool He has

a pool float and goggles He jumps into

the pool and feels the Cool water on his

skin. when sam gets out of the pool, it is

145 p.m

amy did not do her math homework.

right after schol, a friend came over, and

they watched a show. At 430, she baked

an Apple Pie for that night's dessert After

diner, amy was slepy, so she turned out

the light and went to bed early

Unit 4 • Paragraph 15 Errors

Capitalization	5
Colons	1
Periods	2
Spelling	3

Total Errors: 11

it is 1230 p.m. It is hot and sunny.

sam is going to play in the pool He has

a pool float and goggles He jumps into

the pool and feels the Cool water on his

skin. when sam gets out of the pool, it is

145 p.m

Unit 4 • Paragraph 16 Errors

Capitalization	5
Colons	2
Periods	3

Total Errors: 10

Bill pickett was a famous rodeo star.

He was born around december 5 1870.

Bill waz only ten yers old when he

began working as a cowboy He was one

of the best steer wrestlers ever. Some

say bill pickett invented steer wrestling

Mr and mrs Martinez have a new baby.

He was born on thursday september 30.

They hav named him Carlo Martinez, Jr.

There will be a party on saturday october

9, at his grandparents' hous to welcome

little carlo

Bill pickett was a famous rodeo star.

He was born around december 5, 1870.

Bill ~~waz~~ *was* only ten yers old when he

began working as a cowboy. He was one

of the best steer wrestlers ever. Some

say bill pickett invented steer wrestling.

Unit 5 • Paragraph 17
Errors

Capitalization	4
Commas	1
Periods	2
Spelling	2

Total Errors: 9

Mr. and mrs. Martinez have a new baby.

He was born on thursday, september 30.

They hav named him Carlo Martinez, Jr.

There will be a party on saturday, october

9, at his grandparents' hous to welcome

little carlo.

Unit 5 • Paragraph 18
Errors

Capitalization	6
Commas	2
Periods	3
Spelling	2

Total Errors: 13

Helen keller was born June 27 1880, in tuscumbia Alabama. When she was a toddler, she became sick. helen keller was left blind, deaf, and mute She was taught to speak and to reade and write in braille. helen keller wrote boks and gave talks.

Ther are som old cities under the ground in Turkey. One is derinkuyu turkey. Some of the cities are over 2,000 years old. No One lives in these cities today, but peopl still visit them

Helen keller was born June 27, 1880, in tuscumbia, Alabama. When she was a toddler, she became sick. helen keller was left blind, deaf, and mute. She was taught to speak and to reade and write in braille. helen keller wrote boks and gave talks.

Unit 5 • Paragraph 19 Errors

Capitalization 6
Commas 2
Periods 1
Spelling 2

Total Errors: 11

Ther are som old cities under the ground in Turkey. One is derinkuyu, turkey. Some of the cities are over 2,000 years old. No One lives in these cities today, but peopl still visit them.

Unit 5 • Paragraph 20 Errors

Capitalization 3
Commas 1
Periods 1
Spelling 3

Total Errors: 8

We went to our grandparents' house for thanksgiving. There was a lot of food. There were rolls turkey Cranberry sauce stuffing and potatoes. For dessert, there were pies cakes candies and ice cream. We all ate until we were stuffed

rocks on Earth's surface r always wearing away. Rain ice wind and moving water make little pieces break off. these pieces can settle on the rock. Later, more rok pieces covr them. in this way, layer after layer builds up

We went to our grandparents' house for thanksgiving. There was a lot of food. There were rolls, turkey, Cranberry sauce, stuffing, and potatoes. For dessert, there were pies, cakes, candies, and ice cream. We all ate until we were stuffed.

Unit 6 • Paragraph 21
Errors

Capitalization 2
Commas 7
Periods 1

Total Errors: 10

rocks on Earth's surface are always wearing away. Rain, ice, wind, and moving water make little pieces break off. these pieces can settle on the rock. Later, more rok pieces covr them. in this way, layer after layer builds up.

Unit 6 • Paragraph 22
Errors

Capitalization 3
Commas 3
Periods 1
Spelling 3

Total Errors: 10

the clase was planning a partee. The students wanted to hav cookies fruit and punch. the students would also need plates cups and napkins. The students made a list of items and gave it to the teacher

Babe ruth was a baseball player. He was on three teams. He playd for the red sox, the yankees, and the braves. His coach called him "Babe." Babe hit 60 home runs in one year he is in the Baseball Hall of Fame.

the ~~clase~~ was planning a ~~partee~~. The
students wanted to hav cookies, fruit, and
punch. the students would also need plates,
cups, and napkins. The students made a
list of items and gave it to the teacher.

class *party* *e*

Unit 6 • Paragraph 23 Errors	
Capitalization	2
Commas........	4
Periods........	1
Spelling	3

Total Errors: 10

Babe ruth was a baseball player. He
was on three teams. He playd for the red
sox, the yankees, and the braves. His coach
called him "Babe." Babe hit 60 home runs
in one year, he is in the Baseball Hall
of Fame.

Unit 6 • Paragraph 24 Errors	
Capitalization	6
Periods.........	1
Spelling	1

Total Errors: 8

One day, an monkey found a orange

and a carrot in an old shed. it gave the

orange to an apes in a tree. then, it put

the carrot in a empty box to save for

later. An hungry fox found the carrot and

took it to his lair under a old oak tree

What kinds of animals have whiskers

Cats mice and seal have whiskers. Other

animal have whiskers, too a cats just has

a few whiskers An walrus can have more

than 500 whisker.

One day, an monkey found a[n] orange and a carrot in an old shed. it gave the orange to an apes in a tree. then, it put the carrot in a[n] empty box to save for later. An hungry fox found the carrot and took it to his lair under a[n] old oak tree.

Unit 7 • Paragraph 25
Errors

Capitalization	2
Periods	1
Plurals	1
Usage	5

Total Errors: 9

What kinds of animals have whiskers[?] Cats, mice, and seal[s] have whiskers. Other animal[s] have whiskers, too. a cats just has a few whiskers. An walrus can have more than 500 whisker[s].

Unit 7 • Paragraph 26
Errors

Capitalization	1
Commas	2
Periods	2
Plurals	4
Usage	1
Question Marks	1

Total Errors: 11

a carpenter helps build homes offices, and store. a carpenters uses a tool belt In his tool belt, the carpenter carries a hammer and some nails. Sometimes an carpenter has to climb a ladders to reach the top of an building

Have you ever held an snake Their bodies are covered with scale. snakes are cold-blooded They swallow their foods whole and shed their skin wen it gets too tight

a carpenter helps build homes offices, and store. a carpenters uses a tool belt In his tool belt, the carpenter carries a hammer and some nails. Sometimes a carpenter has to climb a ladders to reach the top of a building

Unit 7 • Paragraph 27 Errors

Capitalization 2
Commas. 1
Periods. 2
Plurals 3
Usage 2

Total Errors: 10

Have you ever held a snake Their bodies are covered with scale. snakes are cold-blooded They swallow their foods whole and shed their skin wen it gets too tight

Unit 7 • Paragraph 28 Errors

Capitalization 1
Periods. 2
Plurals 2
Spelling 1
Usage 1
Question Marks . . 1

Total Errors: 8

sharks live dep in the ocean They do

not have bones. they have cartilage. It is

the same thing you hav in your nose and

ears. their tooths are sharp like knifes.

Sometimes they lose one teeth, and an new

one will grow right back in

my parents promised to get me an pet

of my own We got in the car and drove

to the pet store. With the other childs, i

looked at a goose a bird and a mice. I

finally decided to get an brown hamster

with three white feet

sharks live dep in the ocean. They do not have bones. they have cartilage. It is the same thing you hav in your nose and ears. their tooths are sharp like knifes. Sometimes they lose one teeth, and a new one will grow right back in.

**Unit 8 • Paragraph 29
Errors**

Capitalization 3
Periods. 2
Plurals 3
Spelling 2
Usage 1

Total Errors: 11

my parents promised to get me a pet of my own. We got in the car and drove to the pet store. With the other childs, i looked at a goose, a bird, and a mice. I finally decided to get a brown hamster with three white feet.

**Unit 8 • Paragraph 30
Errors**

Capitalization 2
Commas. 2
Periods. 2
Plurals 2
Usage 2

Total Errors: 10

Fish have scales on their bodys. They have gill on the sides of their bodies. These gills look lik small slits These small slits open and close. They help the Fish to breathe in the water. the fins help the fish move around in the watr.

some people are scared of mouses. On a TV program, a man jumped on a table when he saw a mice. however, some children like mice and keep them as pets Would you like to have a mouse for a pet, or would you be scareded

Fish have scales on their ~~bodys.~~ bodies They

have gill on the sides of their bodies. These

gills look lik small slits These small slits

open and close. They help the Fish to

breathe in the water. the fins help the

fish move around in the watr.

**Unit 8 • Paragraph 31
Errors**

Capitalization 2
Periods 1
Plurals 1
Spelling 3

Total Errors: 7

some people are scared of ~~mouses.~~ mice

On a TV program, a man jumped on a

table when he saw a ~~mice.~~ mouse however, some

children like mice and keep them as pets

Would you like to have a mouse for a

pet, or would you be ~~scareded~~ scared ?

**Unit 8 • Paragraph 32
Errors**

Capitalization 2
Periods 1
Plurals 2
Spelling 1
Question Marks . . 1

Total Errors: 7

robert and dale were having a campout

in roberts back yard. The boys heard an

noise outside the tent. They heard the

noise again! It was closer now. What

could it be Al of a sudden, roberts dog

came around the corner

It was Grandmas birtday She went out

to check the mail. There was not even an

card. She wondered if everyone had

forgotten. still puzzled, she came ovr to

Moms house. "Surprise!" yelled the whole

family. we hade been hiding and waiting

robert and dale were having a campout

in roberts back yard. The boys heard an

noise outside the tent. They heard the

noise again! It was closer now. What

could it be Al of a sudden, roberts dog

came around the corner

Unit 9 • Paragraph 33 Errors

Apostrophes 2
Capitalization 4
Periods 1
Spelling 1
Usage 1
Question Marks . . 1

Total Errors: 10

It was Grandmas birtday She went out

to check the mail. There was not even an

card. She wondered if everyone had

forgotten. still puzzled, she came ovr to

Moms house. "Surprise!" yelled the whole

family. we hade been hiding and waiting

Unit 9 • Paragraph 34 Errors

Apostrophes 2
Capitalization 2
Periods 2
Spelling 3
Usage 1

Total Errors: 10

A elephants nos is called a trunk The

elephant uses it to spray mud on its skin

on hote days. An trunk can also grab

things breathe and hold water. the

elephants is one of the worlds most

interesting animals

Lee wished he could liv in the trees

like the birds Lee built himself an tree

house. the birds liked Lees new tree

hous. They built nests in lee's tree The

sparrows nests is closest to his house

A elephants nos is called a trunk. The elephant uses it to spray mud on its skin on hote days. An trunk can also grab things breathe and hold water. the elephants is one of the worlds most interesting animals.

Unit 9 • Paragraph 35 Errors

Apostrophes 2
Capitalization 1
Commas 2
Periods 2
Plurals 1
Spelling 2
Usage 2

Total Errors: 12

Lee wished he could liv in the trees like the birds. Lee built himself an tree house. the birds liked Lees new tree hous. They built nests in lee's tree. The sparrows nests is closest to his house.

Unit 9 • Paragraph 36 Errors

Apostrophes 2
Capitalization 2
Periods 3
Plurals 1
Spelling 2
Usage 1

Total Errors: 11

Me am going to Grandmas house. Us are going to bake cookies. Us will also pop popcorn. Grandma will rent a scary movie Later, us will sit outside under the moon. we will look at the stars. if I see a falling star, me will make a weesh.

sam went to bed He was dreaming about space. Him sat up in his bed and looked all around He was not in his beds. he was wearing an puffy white suit. Him had glove on his hands and big boots on his foot. He was in space!

I
~~Me~~ am going to Grandma's house. ~~Us~~ We
are going to bake cookies. ~~Us~~ We will also
pop popcorn. Grandma will rent a scary
movie. Later, ~~us~~ we will sit outside under the
moon. we will look at the stars. if I see
a falling star, ~~me~~ I will make a ~~weesh.~~ wish.

Unit 10 • Paragraph 37
Errors

Apostrophes 1
Capitalization 2
Periods 1
Pronouns 5
Spelling 1

Total Errors: 10

sam went to bed. He was dreaming
about space. ~~Him~~ He sat up in his bed and
looked all around. He was not in his beds.
he was wearing a puffy white suit. ~~Him~~ He
had glove s on his hands and big boots on
his ~~foot.~~ feet. He was in space!

Unit 10 • Paragraph 38
Errors

Capitalization 2
Periods 2
Plurals 3
Pronouns 2
Usage 1

Total Errors: 10

penguins are unusual birds Them hav feathers, but them cannot fly. They spend most of their time swimming. the water is where penguins find their food. Them really enjoy eating fish squid and krill

Unit 10
Paragraph
39

heidi and I saved up our moneys for a long time Finally, us asked my mom to take we to the mall. i bought meself an shert with the money i had saved. Heidi bought himself a bracelet. Then we got ourselves ice cream

Unit 10
Paragraph
40

penguins are unusual birds. Them hav[e] ^They^

feathers, but them cannot fly. They spend ^they^

most of their time swimming. the water

is where penguins find their food. Them ^They^

really enjoy eating fish, squid, and krill.

**Unit 10 • Paragraph 39
Errors**

Capitalization 2
Commas 2
Periods 2
Pronouns 3
Spelling 1

Total Errors: 10

heidi and I saved up our moneys for

a long time. Finally, us asked my mom to ^we^

take we to the mall. i bought meself an ^us^ ^myself^

shert with the money i had saved. Heidi ^shirt^

bought himself a bracelet. Then we got ^herself^

ourselves ice cream.

**Unit 10 • Paragraph 40
Errors**

Capitalization 3
Periods 2
Plurals 1
Pronouns 4
Spelling 1
Usage 1

Total Errors: 12

Mary and may are best friends Every
afternoon, the girls do their homework
together. They munch on Mays favorite
snack, grapes. Then, mary and may goes
to the park. Mary takes her skates. May
bring her scooter

Each morning, al sweeps the steps. Him
keeps them nice and clean. Al also feed
the goats Them are hapy to see him
coming. Then, Al stop and watches the
sunrise with the farm animal. They all
watches together. the roosters crow.

Mary and may are best friends. Every

afternoon, the girls do their homework

together. They munch on Mays favorite

snack, grapes. Then, mary and may ~~goes~~ go

to the park. Mary takes her skates. May

bring her scooter.

**Unit 11 • Paragraph 41
Errors**

Apostrophes. 1
Capitalization 3
Periods. 2
Verbs 2

Total Errors: 8

Each morning, al sweeps the steps. ~~Him~~ He

keeps them nice and clean. Al also feed

the goats. ~~Them~~ They are hapy to see him

coming. Then, Al stop and watches the

sunrise with the farm animal. They all

watches together. the roosters crow.

**Unit 11 • Paragraph 42
Errors**

Capitalization 2
Periods. 1
Plurals 1
Pronouns 2
Spelling 1
Verbs 3

Total Errors: 10

our school are great! Our school colors

is green orange and black. our school

mascot are the lion We have an football

team, an softball team, and a basketball

teams. Us also have craft classes like

painting ceramics and photography

Emperor penguins lives in cold

antarctica. Like other burds, penguins lay

eggs. The female Emperor penguin lays a

egg. the male penguin balance it on his

foots for six long weeks. Him has an flap

of skin that covers the egg and keeps

it warm

our school ~~are~~ [is] great! Our school colors

[are] ~~is~~ green, orange, and black. our school

mascot ~~are~~ [is] the lion. We have an football

team, an softball team, and a basketball

teams. ~~Us~~ [We] also have craft classes like

painting, ceramics, and photography.

Unit 11 • Paragraph 43
Errors

Capitalization 2
Commas. 4
Periods. 2
Plurals 1
Pronouns 1
Usage 2
Verbs 3

Total Errors: 15

Emperor penguins lives in cold

antarctica. Like other ~~burds~~ [birds], penguins lay

eggs. The female Emperor penguin lays a[n]

egg. the male penguin balance[s] it on his

[feet] ~~foots~~ for six long weeks. ~~Him~~ [He] has an flap

of skin that covers the egg and keeps

it warm.

Unit 11 • Paragraph 44
Errors

Capitalization 2
Periods. 1
Plurals 1
Pronouns 1
Spelling 1
Usage 2
Verbs 2

Total Errors: 10

Name: _____   Date: _____

Manny was at the park Under one trees, a child sat wearing a hat and reading an book. Manny runned over to the slide. Him climbed up and slided down. next, him go to the swings He went very high in the aire.

My family and me like to go camping Last week, we go camping by a rivers. We took along tents and sleeping bags. Us packed food. My mom took we on hikes. my brother rowing an canoe. at night, we roasted marshmallows.

Manny was at the park.Under one

trees, a child sat wearing a hat and reading

aṉ book. Manny ~~runned~~ over to the slide.
(ran)

~~Him~~ climbed up and slided down. next, ~~him~~
(He) (he)

~~go~~ to the swings.He went very high in the
(went)

aire.

Unit 12 • Paragraph 45 Errors

Capitalization 1
Periods 2
Plurals 1
Pronouns 2
Spelling 1
Usage 1
Verbs 3

Total Errors: 11

My family and ~~me~~ like to go camping.
(I)

Last week, we ~~go~~ camping by a rivers.
(went)

We took along tents and sleeping bags. ~~Us~~
(We)

packed food. My mom took ~~we~~ on
(us)

hikes. my brother ~~rowing~~ aṉ canoe. at
(rowed)

night, we roasted marshmallows.

Unit 12 • Paragraph 46 Errors

Capitalization 2
Periods 1
Plurals 1
Pronouns 3
Usage 1
Verbs 2

Total Errors: 10

long ago, many schools in the united States haved only one rom All the grades were together Boys and girls sat on opposite sides of the room. The smaller childs sitted in front, and the older childs sitted in back.

andy wants to hit an home run at his next baseball game Each day, he practices baseball with his dad. Him tries really hard. as his next game gets closer, andy worry, but he believes he can hit an home run

long ago, many schools in the united

had   o
States ~~haved~~ only one rom. All the grades

were together. Boys and girls sat on

opposite sides of the room. The smaller

children   sat
~~childs~~ ~~sitted~~ in front, and the older ~~childs~~ children

sat
~~sitted~~ in back.

Unit 12 • Paragraph 47 Errors

Capitalization	2
Periods.	2
Plurals	2
Spelling	1
Verbs	3

Total Errors: 10

andy wants to hit a home run at his

next baseball game. Each day, he practices

He
baseball with his dad. ~~Him~~ tries really

hard. as his next game gets closer, andy

worries
~~worry,~~ but he believes he can hit a

home run.

Unit 12 • Paragraph 48 Errors

Capitalization	3
Periods.	2
Pronouns	1
Usage	2
Verbs	1

Total Errors: 9

I dont like soda Its bubbles make my throat and noses feal funny. When Im finished drinking an soda, i burp. sometimes when I opens an can, it spray all over the plac. I think Ill just drink water.

Haley was picking out a stuffed animal. She looked at a bunny. It wasnt what she wanted. She didnt want an zebras either Then her saw it! With its black and white fur, it were the cutest thing in the store. Haley knew that her wanted that panda

I dont like soda Its bubbles make my

throat and noses feel funny. When Im

finished drinking a soda, i burp.

sometimes when I opens a can, it spray

all over the plac. I think Ill just drink

water.

Unit 13 • Paragraph 49 Errors

Apostrophes	3
Capitalization	2
Periods	1
Plurals	1
Spelling	2
Usage	2
Verbs	2

Total Errors: 13

Haley was picking out a stuffed animal.

She looked at a bunny. It wasnt what she

wanted. She didnt want a zebras either

Then her saw it! With its black and white

fur, it were the cutest thing in the store.

Haley knew that her wanted that panda

Unit 13 • Paragraph 50 Errors

Apostrophes	2
Periods	2
Plurals	1
Pronouns	2
Usage	1
Verbs	1

Total Errors: 9

Jennys room was so messy, her couldnt even find she socs! Her mother suggested they have a Great Sock Hunt Theyd put clothes in an basket. all the sock would be greeted with cheers and awarded points. The prize would be a clene rooms.

Unit 13
Paragraph
51

Little ana was sure there was something under her bedd. Her brother danny said there wasnt, but by then shed started crying. Danny liftd up the quilt. Suddenly, him shrieked. Out hopped Dannys frog, whod escaped that morning.

Unit 13
Paragraph
52

Jenny's room was so messy, ~~her~~ *she* couldn't

even find ~~she~~ *her* soc*k*s! Her mother suggested

they have a Great Sock Hunt. They'd put

clothes in a*n* basket. all the sock*s* would

be greeted with cheers and awarded

points. The prize would be a ~~clene~~ *clean* rooms.

Little ana was sure there was something

under her bed. Her brother danny said

there wasn't, but by then she'd started

crying. Danny lift*e*d up the quilt. Suddenly,

~~him~~ *he* shrieked. Out hopped Danny's frog,

who'd escaped that morning.

I love to flie! It's really fun when the plane takes off. I can gets too Grandmas house really fast in a airplane. in the car, it takes ate ours. When i grow up, i want to bee an airplane pilot and sea the whole worlds from above.

Which for states can a person stand in at the same time Which four states have borders that touch The for state are arizona, colorado, new Mexico, and utah. The corners of these state all meeting at won point.

I love to ~~flie!~~ fly It's really fun when the plane takes off. I can gets too Grandmas house really fast in a airplane. in the car, it takes ~~ate~~ eight ours. When i grow up, i want to bee an airplane pilot and ~~sea~~ see the whole worlds from above.

Unit 14 • Paragraph 53
Errors

Apostrophes 1
Capitalization 3
Homophones 5
Plurals 1
Spelling 1
Usage 1
Verbs 1

Total Errors: 13

Which for states can a person stand in at the same time Which four states have borders that touch The for state are arizona, colorado, new Mexico, and utah. The corners of these state all meeting at ~~won~~ one point.

Unit 14 • Paragraph 54
Errors

Capitalization 4
Homophones 3
Plurals 2
Question Marks . . 2
Verbs 1

Total Errors: 12

~~~~~~

camping is fun four many reason. Food

tastes better when it is cooked over a

open fire. Me like too hike in the woods

and catch fishes in the river. At the end

of the day, me like too sleep in an

cozy sleeping bag

~~~~~~

have you ever seen an chipmunk with

very fat cheeks The fat cheeks make it

easy for chipmunks too carry food too their

homes All Day, the chipmunks run around

and look four items such as acorns seeds

and berrys.

camping is fun ~~four~~ *for* many reason*s*. Food

tastes better when it is cooked over a*n*

open fire. ~~Me~~ *I* like too* hike in the woods

and catch fishe*s* in the river. At the end

of the day, ~~me~~ *I* like too* sleep in an*

cozy sleeping bag*.*

**Unit 14 • Paragraph 55
Errors**

Capitalization 1
Homophones 3
Periods 1
Plurals 2
Pronouns 2
Usage 2

Total Errors: 11

have you ever seen an* chipmunk with

very fat cheeks*?* The fat cheeks make it

easy for chipmunks too* carry food too* their

homes*.* All *D*ay, the chipmunks run around

and look ~~four~~ *for* items such as acorns*,* seeds*,*

and ~~berrys.~~ *berries*

**Unit 14 • Paragraph 56
Errors**

Capitalization 2
Commas 2
Homophones 3
Periods 1
Plurals 1
Question Marks . . 1
Usage 1

Total Errors: 11

Hannah learned about cherry blossoms.

She learn that when them are in bloom, an

tiny breeze can send their petals drifting

through the air Hannah decided too write

an pome called warm snow about cherry

blossom.

marcus and his mother looked down

the long street too their left. They could

hear an song called hoedown being played.

Then the band marchd around a corners.

There they were! The musicians wore

bright yellow uniforms and played as

them marched

Hannah learned about cherry blossoms.

She learn~~ed~~ that when ~~them~~ *they* are in bloom, a~~n~~ tiny breeze can send their petals drifting through the air⊙ Hannah decided to~~o~~ write a~~n~~ ~~pome~~ *poem* called "warm snow" about cherry blossom.^s

Unit 15 • Paragraph 57
Errors

Capitalization 2
Homophones 1
Periods. 1
Plurals 1
Pronouns 1
Quotation Marks. . 2
Spelling 1
Usage 2
Verbs 1

Total Errors: 12

marcus and his mother looked down the long street to~~o~~ their left. They could hear a~~n~~ song called "hoedown" being played. Then the band marchd around a corners⊙ There they were! The musicians wore bright yellow uniforms and played as ~~them~~ *they* marched⊙

Unit 15 • Paragraph 58
Errors

Capitalization 2
Homophones 1
Periods. 1
Plurals 1
Pronouns 1
Quotation Marks. . 2
Usage 1
Verbs 1

Total Errors: 10

I like to cooks. Me like too create new

dishes like peanut butter burritos Last

night, I maked chocolate spaghetti. No

one in my family will try anything that

me makes, but I lov my creations. Im

going to write an cookbook and call it

Yummy Mistakes

Mail carriers deliver the mal. They

delivers leters postcards magazines and

package. Our mail carrier is named tracy.

Even if its raining, she still does the job!

I always know that Ill get my favorite

magazine, goofy pets, on time.

I like to cooks. Me like too create new

dishes like peanut butter burritos. Last

night, I ~~maked~~ (made) chocolate spaghetti. No

one in my family will try anything that

me makes, but I lov my creations. Im

going to write a cookbook and call it

Yummy Mistakes.

**Unit 15 • Paragraph 59
Errors**

Apostrophes 1
Homophones 1
Periods 2
Pronouns 2
Spelling 1
Underlines 1
Usage 1
Verbs 3

Total Errors: 12

Mail carriers deliver the mal. They

delivers leters, postcards, magazines, and

package. Our mail carrier is named tracy.

Even if its raining, she still does the job!

I always know that Ill get my favorite

magazine, goofy pets, on time.

**Unit 15 • Paragraph 60
Errors**

Apostrophes 2
Capitalization 3
Commas 3
Plurals 1
Spelling 2
Underlines 1
Verbs 1

Total Errors: 13

I have an very sleepy cat. She can fall asleep anywhere. Won time, her felled asleep inside my dads boot. Yesterday, she crawled into my sock drawer and slept there all days! We changed she name from frisky too sleepy.

How fast does sound travel through air It goes about 700 mile per hour. What iff something go faster than sound We say that it braked the sond barrier. When something breaks the sound barrier, we here something. We hear an sonic boom.

I have an very sleepy cat. She can

fall asleep anywhere. Won time, her felled

asleep inside my dads boot. Yesterday, she

crawled into my sock drawer and slept

there all days! We changed she name

from frisky too sleepy.

**Unit 16 • Paragraph 61
Errors**

Apostrophes 1
Capitalization 2
Homophones 2
Plurals 1
Pronouns 2
Usage 1
Verbs 1

Total Errors: 10

How fast does sound travel through air

It goes about 700 mile per hour. What if

something go faster than sound We say

that it braked the sond barrier. When

something breaks the sound barrier, we

here something. We hear an sonic boom.

**Unit 16 • Paragraph 62
Errors**

Homophones 1
Plurals 1
Question Marks . . 2
Spelling 2
Usage 1
Verbs 2

Total Errors: 9

Name: _____ Date: _____

Kelly was cleaning her room. She found

three buttons and a old sock that had a

whole in it. She decided to use these

thing to make an puppet. She carried the

sok and butons to her mother her mother

helped her make the puppet.

Meg and her father gotting into an

small bote and paddled out past the pier.

The wind was strong and made big waves.

Meg felt sik. At last, they got back to the

lands. Meg decided that nex time, her

would wait for an calm day

Kelly was cleaning her room. She found

three buttons and a(n) old sock that had a

whole in it. She decided to use these

thing(s) to make a(n) puppet. She carried the

sok and butons to her mother. her mother

helped her make the puppet.

Unit 16 • Paragraph 63
Errors

Capitalization 1
Homophones 1
Periods 1
Plurals 1
Spelling 2
Usage 2

Total Errors: 8

Meg and her father gotting(got) into a(n)

small bote(boat) and paddled out past the pier.

The wind was strong and made big waves.

Meg felt sik. At last, they got back to the

lands. Meg decided that next time, her(she)

would wait for a(n) calm day.

Unit 16 • Paragraph 64
Errors

Periods 1
Plurals 1
Pronouns 1
Spelling 3
Usage 2
Verbs 1

Total Errors: 9

Umbrellas come in all sizes. Them come in all color. Some people use they in the rain. Others use them when it are hot. Some has umbrelas just four fun. umbrellas have many use!

My grandma and grampa loves too see the fal colors. Each year, they travel along the East Coast. Them have a bige book called east coast atlas that they use to plan their trips.

Umbrellas come in all sizes. ~~Them~~ They come in all color~~s~~. Some people use ~~they~~ them in the rain. Others use them when it ~~are~~ is hot.

Some ~~has~~ have umbrel~~l~~as just ~~four~~ for fun. _umbrellas_ have many use~~s~~!

Unit 17 • Paragraph 65
Errors

Capitalization	1
Homophones	1
Plurals	2
Pronouns	2
Spelling	1
Verbs	2

Total Errors: 9

My grandma and ~~grampa~~ grandpa loves~~s~~ to~~o~~ see the fal~~l~~ colors. Each year, they travel along the East Coast. ~~Them~~ They have a big~~e~~ book called east coast atlas that they use to plan their trips.

Unit 17 • Paragraph 66
Errors

Capitalization	3
Homophones	1
Pronouns	1
Spelling	3
Underlines	1
Verbs	1

Total Errors: 10

Grasslands covr parts of africa. Zebras elephants lions and leopard live there. You can reads about aminals that live in grasslands. You can find books at the library, or you cane find websites

Tomorrow, I will play with Grandmas neu kittens I will throwing a bal for her dog. I hope me get to ride her horse. I like going to Grandmas house

Grasslands covr parts of africa. Zebras
e

elephants lions and leopard live there.
s

You can reads about aminals that live in
animals

grasslands. You can find books at the

library, or you cane find websites

**Unit 17 • Paragraph 67
Errors**

Capitalization 1
Commas. 3
Periods. 1
Plurals 1
Spelling 3
Verbs 1

Total Errors: 10

Tomorrow, I will play with Grandmas

neu kittens I will throwing a bal for her
new

dog. I hope me get to ride her horse. I
I

like going to Grandmas house

**Unit 17 • Paragraph 68
Errors**

Apostrophes. 2
Periods. 2
Pronouns 1
Spelling 2
Verbs 1

Total Errors: 8

Electricity is important We nede it to

turn on lights. Us use it to toast bredd. We

needs it four hour computers. we use it

to wach TV. When you plug somethings

in, you use electricity

Families from many citys were at the

county fair. At the fair, the pigs were in

the pigpen. Ther were horse in the barn.

There were also ladies dressed as Fairies.

Them were sell juice candy and berry pies

Electricity is important. We ~~nede~~ (need) **it to turn on lights.** ~~Us~~ (We) **use it to toast** ~~bredd~~ (bread). **We** needs̶ **it** ~~four hour~~ (for our) **computers.** we **use it to wach (watch) TV. When you plug somethings̶ (something) in, you use electricity.**

Unit 18 • Paragraph 69
Errors

Capitalization 1
Homophones 2
Periods 2
Plurals 1
Pronouns 1
Spelling 3
Verbs 1

Total Errors: 11

Families from many ~~citys~~ (cities) **were at the county fair. At the fair, the pigs were in the pigpen. Ther** (There) **were horse s (horses) in the barn. There were also ladies dressed as F̶airies. ** ~~Them~~ (They) **were sell ing (selling) juice, candy, and berry pies.**

Unit 18 • Paragraph 70
Errors

Capitalization 1
Commas 2
Periods 1
Plurals 2
Pronouns 1
Spelling 1
Verbs 1

Total Errors: 9

Koalas life in australia They have too thumb on each han. This helps they climb tres. Them can grab branches and hang on tight.

Walt and i are best friends. We met when us wer in kindergarten. Walt liked the color green, and so did me. He liked peanut buter, and I likd jely. Our moms said that us were like to peas in a pod

Koalas ~~life~~ (live) in australia. They have ~~too~~ (two)

thumb (s) on each han (d). This helps ~~they~~ (them) climb

tres (e). ~~Them~~ (They) can grab branches and hang

on tight.

Unit 18 • Paragraph 71
Errors

Capitalization 1
Homophones 1
Periods 1
Plurals 1
Pronouns 2
Spelling 2
Verbs 1

Total Errors: 9

Walt and i (I) are best friends. We met

when ~~us~~ (we) wer (e) in kindergarten. Walt liked

the color green, and so did ~~me~~ (I). He liked

peanut buter (t), and I likd (e) jely (l). Our moms

said that ~~us~~ (we) were like to (w) peas in a pod.

Unit 18 • Paragraph 72
Errors

Capitalization 1
Homophones 1
Periods 1
Pronouns 3
Spelling 2
Verbs 2

Total Errors: 10

A teacher go to school every dae. Her

helps boys and girls learn to read write

and do math. She reads stories too the

students She teaches them new songs.

An teacher love beaing around the boys

and girl.

Ellie is running around the hous. She

is look for her litle brother, scott. Him

is in his hidding place. Ellies face has

an huge smile on it. This is there

favorite game.

A teacher go(es) to school every ~~dae~~(day). ~~Her~~(She)
helps boys and girls learn to read(,) write(,)
and do math. She reads stories to(o) the
students(.) She teaches them new songs.
A(ll) teacher love(s) ~~beaing~~(being) around the boys
and girl(s).

Unit 19 • Paragraph 73 Errors

Commas	2
Homophones	1
Periods	1
Plurals	1
Pronouns	1
Spelling	2
Usage	1
Verbs	2

Total Errors: 11

Ellie is running around the hous(e). She
is look(ing) for her li(t)le brother, scott. ~~Him~~(He)
is in his ~~hidding~~(hiding) place. Ellie(')s face has
a(n) huge smile on it. This is ~~there~~(their)
favorite game.

Unit 19 • Paragraph 74 Errors

Apostrophes	1
Capitalization	1
Homophones	1
Pronouns	1
Spelling	3
Usage	1
Verbs	1

Total Errors: 9

Kates mom bought she an strawberry ice-cream cone after lunches. Kate enjoyd eating the ice cream as they walked through the park. When kate was finished with her ice-cream cone, her said, "Thank you for the special tret, Mom!"

In the meadow, you will find many animals, including the harvest mous. This tiny animal can climb from plant too plant Harvest mouses climb these plant looking for foods. Them eat as much as they can in the Summer to getting ready for winter

Kate's mom bought ~~she~~ her an strawberry ice-cream cone after lunches. Kate enjoyd eating the ice cream as they walked through the park. When kate was finished with her ice-cream cone, ~~her~~ she said, "Thank you for the special tret, Mom!"

Unit 19 • Paragraph 75 Errors

Apostrophes. 1
Capitalization 1
Plurals 1
Pronouns 2
Spelling 1
Usage 1
Verbs 1

Total Errors: 8

In the meadow, you will find many animals, including the harvest mous. This tiny animal can climb from plant too plant. Harvest ~~mouses~~ mice climb these plant looking for foods. ~~Them~~ They eat as much as they can in the Summer to getting ready for winter.

Unit 19 • Paragraph 76 Errors

Capitalization 1
Homophones 1
Periods. 2
Plurals 3
Pronouns 1
Spelling 1
Verbs 1

Total Errors: 10

We have a very scary vacuum cleaners. It makes an scary, roaring nois. It chases I around the house It has a light on it that loks like a eye. Me refuse to vacuum my rume!

Unlike its cousins in India, the African elephant has big, floppy ear. it likes to hang out wit its heard on th grasslands. It is purty peaceful, but if it is annoyed, it wil charges!

We have a very scary vacuum cleaners.

It makes an scary, roaring nois. It chases

me
I around the house. It has a light on it

that loks like a eye. Me refuse to vacuum

room
my rume!

Unit 20 • Paragraph 77
Errors

Periods.........	1
Plurals.........	1
Pronouns.......	2
Spelling........	3
Usage..........	2

Total Errors: 9

Unlike its cousins in India, the African

s
elephant has big, floppy ear. it likes to

h   herd   e
hang out wit its heard on th grasslands.

pretty
It is purty peaceful, but if it is annoyed,

l
it wil charges!

Unit 20 • Paragraph 78
Errors

Capitalization	1
Homophones	1
Plurals.........	1
Spelling........	4
Verbs..........	1

Total Errors: 8

I luve to play after school with mindy and heather. Sometimes us jump rope on Heathers big, smooth driveway. Somtimes we goes to my house and play dolls with my litel sisters. We play until 430 p.m. Then we half too do homework.

I love crayons. There are indigo and lime crayon. There are even crayons that smelling lik watermelons and blueberries! Even when they dont smell like fruit, I like how them smell. That waxy smell means me get two draw some new picture.

I ~~luve~~ *love* to play after school with mindy
and heather. Sometimes ~~us~~ *we* jump rope on
Heathers big, smooth driveway. Somtimes
we goes to my house and play dolls with
my ~~litel~~ *little* sisters. We play until 430 p.m.
Then we ~~half~~ too *have* do homework.

Unit 20 • Paragraph 79
Errors

Apostrophes 1
Capitalization 2
Colons 1
Homophones 2
Pronouns 1
Spelling 3
Verbs 1

Total Errors: 11

I love crayons. There are indigo and
lime crayon. There are even crayons that
~~smelling~~ *lik* watermelons and blueberries!
Even when they dont smell like fruit, I like
how ~~them~~ *they* smell. That waxy smell means
~~me~~ *I* get ~~two~~ *to* draw some new picture.

Unit 20 • Paragraph 80
Errors

Apostrophes 1
Homophones 1
Plurals 2
Pronouns 2
Spelling 1
Verbs 1

Total Errors: 8

My favorit animals are dolphins. Theyre

very smart. Dolphins are mammals I also

like chimpanzees. Them are smart, two.

Do you know what chimpanzees eat They

likes to eat plants meat and insect.

Can you guess how the dead Sea got

its name The watr in the dead See is

sew salty that amost nothing can live in it.

Its water have a higher salt content thann

the oceans!

My favorit^e **animals are dolphins. Theyre**

very smart. Dolphins are mammals. I also

like chimpanzees. ~~Them~~ They **are smart, ~~two~~** too**.**

Do you know what chimpanzees eat ? **They**

likes to eat plants, meat, and insect^s**.**

Unit 21 • Paragraph 81 Errors

Apostrophes..... 1
Commas......... 2
Homophones 1
Periods......... 1
Plurals 1
Pronouns 1
Question Marks .. 1
Spelling 1
Verbs 1

Total Errors: 10

Can you guess how the dead Sea got

its name ? **The watr in the dead ~~See~~** Sea **is**

~~sew~~ so **salty that amost nothing can live in it.**

Its water ~~have~~ has **a higher salt content thann**

the oceans!

Unit 21 • Paragraph 82 Errors

Capitalization 2
Homophones 2
Question Marks .. 1
Spelling 3
Verbs 1

Total Errors: 9

Won day, mike was walking along the stret when he saw sally. She was carrying an puppy in she arms Sally letted Mike pet the puppy. She said her was taking it to skool to show her classmates

Is a snak a scary animal The gras snake likes to rest in the son. Grass snakes eet frog and newts. They lives in marshy meadows Sometimes, the grass snake will pretending to be ded. The more you learn about snakes, the less scary they is.

One
~~Won~~ day, mike was walking along the

e
stret when he saw sally. She was carrying

her
an puppy in ~~she~~ arms. Sally letted Mike

she
pet the puppy. She said ~~her~~ was taking it

school
to ~~skool~~ to show her classmates.

Unit 21 • Paragraph 83
Errors

Capitalization 2
Homophones 1
Periods. 2
Pronouns 2
Spelling 2
Usage. 1
Verbs 1

Total Errors: 11

Is a snak a scary animal The gras

sun
snake likes to rest in the ~~son~~. Grass snakes

eat   s
~~ect~~ frog and newts. They lives in marshy

meadows. Sometimes, the grass snake will

a
pretending to be ded. The more you learn

are
about snakes, the less scary they ~~is~~.

Unit 21 • Paragraph 84
Errors

Homophones 1
Periods. 1
Plurals 1
Question Marks . . 1
Spelling 4
Verbs 3

Total Errors: 11

Jaime got ready two go on an hike with his friends. He packed a water bottle trail mix and a maps. When Jaime meeted his friends at the park, Anas dad reminded everyone too stay together Finally, at 315, they all started down the trale.

what aminals would you want to see first at the zoo Maybe youd want to look way up at the giraffes or way down at the alligators. Maybe youd even want to walk on an special bridge through the tres and looking at birds on the branches nex to you.

Jaime got ready ~~two~~ [to] go on a~~n~~ hike with his friends. He packed a water bottle, trail mix, and a maps. When Jaime ~~meeted~~ [met] his friends at the park, Ana's dad reminded everyone to~~o~~ stay together. Finally, at 315, they all started down the ~~trale.~~ [trail.]

Unit 22 • Paragraph 85 Errors

Apostrophes. 1
Colons 1
Commas. 2
Homophones 2
Periods. 1
Plurals 1
Spelling 1
Usage 1
Verbs 1

Total Errors: 11

what ~~aminals~~ [animals] would you want to see first at the zoo Maybe you'd want to look way up at the giraffes or way down at the alligators. Maybe you'd even want to walk on a~~n~~ special bridge through the tres and look~~ing~~ at birds on the branches nex to you.

Unit 22 • Paragraph 86 Errors

Apostrophes. 2
Capitalization 1
Question Marks . . 1
Spelling 3
Usage 1
Verbs 1

Total Errors: 9

A tale says that atlantis was once an real place. People lived there in beautiful cities. Then won day, it sinked to the bottom of the atlantic ocean. All this took place lon ago. For hundreds of year, peoples have looked for Atlantis

At the beach, Alex found an round, glass ball almost covered with sands. His mother helpd him dig around it. She said that it is an fishermans float. She explained that japanese fishermen once used they to keep their nets frome sinking

A tale says that atlantis was once an
real place. People lived there in beautiful
cities. Then won day, it sinked to the
bottom of the atlantic ocean. All this took
place lon ago. For hundreds of year,
peoples have looked for Atlantis

Unit 22 • Paragraph 87
Errors

Capitalization 3
Homophones 1
Periods 1
Plurals 2
Spelling 1
Usage 1
Verbs 1

Total Errors: 10

At the beach, Alex found an round,
glass ball almost covered with sands. His
mother helpd him dig around it. She said
that it is an fishermans float. She explained
that japanese fishermen once used they to
keep their nets frome sinking

Unit 22 • Paragraph 88
Errors

Apostrophes 1
Capitalization 1
Periods 1
Plurals 1
Pronouns 1
Spelling 1
Usage 2
Verbs 1

Total Errors: 9

Eric and claudia want too work in a hospital when them grow up. They reads books about doctors nurses and the way the body works. Every time they sea doctors or nurses, they asks many question about their jobs

Most ov the time, we sea the moon at night and the son during the day. However, evry once in an while, theres an solar eclipse. the moon passes directly in front of the sun, blocking its light. When this happens, the moons shadow falls on Earth, and suddenly the skies grows dark.

Eric and claudia want too work in a

hospital when ~~them~~ they grow up. They reads

books about doctors, nurses, and the way

the body works. Every time they ~~sea~~ see

doctors or nurses, they asks many

question s about their jobs.

Unit 23 • Paragraph 89 Errors	
Capitalization	1
Commas	2
Homophones	2
Periods	1
Plurals	1
Pronouns	1
Verbs	2

Total Errors: 10

Most ~~ov~~ of the time, we ~~sea~~ see the moon at

night and the ~~son~~ sun during the day. However,

~~evry~~ e once in an while, theres an solar

eclipse. the moon passes directly in front

of the sun, blocking its light. When this

happens, the moons shadow falls on Earth,

and suddenly the ~~skies~~ sky grows dark.

Unit 23 • Paragraph 90 Errors	
Apostrophes	2
Capitalization	1
Homophones	2
Plurals	1
Spelling	2
Usage	2

Total Errors: 10

Maria and her bruder Carl are both

taking swimming lessones. Maria likes the

water and is excited about the lessons.

Carls afraid of the water, but the techer is

patient and nise. She tells carl that each

day he will learn an little more

samuel losted his blew backpack The

last time him remembered seeing his

backpack was on the bus. He askd his

teacher if he could go too the office to

looking for it. When he got there, his

backpacks was waiting for him. Someone

on the bus had brought it two the ofise.

Maria and her ~~bruder~~ *brother* Carl are both

taking swimming ~~lessones.~~ *lessons* Maria likes the

water and is excited about the lessons.

Carls afraid of the water, but the techer is

patient and ~~nise.~~ *nice* She tells carl that each

day he will learn a little more.

Unit 23 • Paragraph 91
Errors

Apostrophes	1
Capitalization	1
Periods	1
Plurals	1
Spelling	3
Usage	1

Total Errors: 8

samuel losted his ~~blew~~ *blue* backpack. The

last time ~~him~~ *he* remembered seeing his

backpack was on the bus. He askd his

teacher if he could go too the office to

looking for it. When he got there, his

backpacks was waiting for him. Someone

on the bus had brought it ~~two~~ *to* the ~~ofise.~~ *office*

Unit 23 • Paragraph 92
Errors

Capitalization	1
Homophones	3
Periods	1
Plurals	1
Pronouns	1
Spelling	1
Verbs	3

Total Errors: 11

Black bears like to liv in forests and swamp areas. Them like too climb tres and swim. Black bears can swim very wel. Black bears like to eating many things. Theyll eat ants bees fish and other animals.

Unit 24
Paragraph 93

Jamaal loved to reed books about space. Him loved to looked up at the mon at night. He new about astronauts. Them explores in Space. Jamaal decided to become a astronaut.

Unit 24
Paragraph 94

Black bears like to live **in forests and swamp areas.** ~~Them~~ They **like to**o **climb tre**e**s and swim. Black bears can swim very wel**l**. Black bears like to eatin**g **many things. They**'**ll **eat ants**,** bees**,** fish**,** and other animals.**

Unit 24 • Paragraph 93 Errors

Apostrophes 1
Commas 3
Homophones 1
Pronouns 1
Spelling 3
Verbs 1

Total Errors: 10

Jamaal loved to ~~reed~~ read **books about space.** ~~Him~~ He **loved to look**e**d up at the mon**o **at night. He** k**new about astronauts.** ~~Them~~ They **explore**s **in** S**pace. Jamaal decided to become a** n **astronaut.**

Unit 24 • Paragraph 94 Errors

Capitalization 1
Homophones 2
Pronouns 2
Spelling 1
Usage 1
Verbs 2

Total Errors: 9

Ben and Pam were running through the house. Their fader said to stop running. All of an sudden, Ben and Pam slid across the floar and felled! They're shirts started to feel damp. What were going on Then them seed the mop buket.

Dwight didn't want to get up four school. All him wanted two do was sleep. Him looked at the clock. It was aready 730! He got ready grabbed his backpack, and went downstairs. His mother look at him and said, "Dwight, why ar you dressed for school It's Saturday!"

Ben and Pam were running through the

house. Their ~~fader~~ *father* **said to stop running.**

All of ~~an~~ **sudden, Ben and Pam slid across**

the ~~floar~~ *floor* **and** ~~felled~~ **!** ~~They're~~ *Their* **shirts started**

to feel damp. What ~~were~~ *was* **going on** *?* **Then**

~~them~~ *they* ~~seed~~ *saw* **the mop bu** *c* **ket.**

Unit 24 • Paragraph 95
Errors

Homophones 1
Pronouns 1
Question Marks . . 1
Spelling 3
Usage 1
Verbs 3

Total Errors: 10

Dwight didn't want to get up ~~four~~ *for*

school. All ~~him~~ *he* **wanted** ~~two~~ *to* **do was sleep.**

~~Him~~ *He* **looked at the clock. It was a** *l* **ready**

: **730! He got ready** *,* **grabbed his backpack,**

and went downstairs. His mother look *ed* **at**

him and said, "Dwight, why ar *e* **you**

dressed for school *?* **It's Saturday!"**

Unit 24 • Paragraph 96
Errors

Colons 1
Commas. 1
Homophones 2
Pronouns 2
Question Marks . . 1
Spelling 2
Verbs 1

Total Errors: 10

Amanda and mark whir walking on the beach. Amanda picked up an shell. Suddenly, her feeled the shell move in her hand. Inside the shell was an small see creature. The shel was its homes. Mark told Amanda two put the animal back in the water

Ralph the raccoon was stuck. his Hand wouldnt come out of the jars Inside his hand was an bright, gren ball. "Let go of the bal," his frend said. Ralph letted go, and his hand was free

Amanda and mark ~~whir~~ _were_ walking on the beach. Amanda picked up an shell. Suddenly, ~~her feeled~~ _she_ _felt_ the shell move in her hand. Inside the shell was an small ~~see~~ _sea_ creature. The shel was its homes. Mark told Amanda ~~two~~ _to_ put the animal back in the water

**Unit 25 • Paragraph 97
Errors**

Capitalization 1
Homophones 3
Periods 1
Plurals 1
Pronouns 1
Spelling 1
Usage 2
Verbs 1

Total Errors: 11

Ralph the raccoon was stuck. his Hand wouldnt come out of the jars Inside his hand was an bright, gren ball. "Let go of the bal," his frend said. Ralph letted go, and his hand was free

**Unit 25 • Paragraph 98
Errors**

Apostrophes 1
Capitalization 2
Periods 2
Plurals 1
Spelling 3
Usage 1
Verbs 1

Total Errors: 11

A Tigers stripes are like your fingerprints. Each tiger has its own stripe pattern. no other tiger have the same pattern. You has your ohn set of fingerprint. No won else has the sam pattern

Snow was falling outside Lane and sam wanted too go outside and playing. Them had know sledes, sew instead of sledding, they builded an snowman.

A *T*igers stripes are like your

fingerprints. Each tiger has its own stripe

pattern. *no* other tiger ~~have~~ *has* the same

pattern. You ~~has~~ *have* your ~~ohn~~ *own* set of

fingerprint*s*. No ~~won~~ *one* else has the sam*e*

pattern*.*

Unit 25 • Paragraph 99
Errors

Apostrophes	1
Capitalization	2
Homophones	1
Periods	1
Plurals	1
Spelling	2
Verbs	2

Total Errors: 10

Snow was falling outside*.* Lane and

*s*am wanted to*o* go outside and play~~ing~~.

~~Them~~ *They* had ~~know~~ *no* ~~sleds~~ *sleds*, ~~sew~~ *so* instead of

sledding, they ~~builded~~ *built* a*n* snowman.

Unit 25 • Paragraph 100
Errors

Capitalization	1
Homophones	3
Periods	1
Plurals	1
Pronouns	1
Usage	1
Verbs	2

Total Errors: 10

Editing Marks

Here is a list of the editing marks that are used in this book.

Mark	Meaning	Example
≡	Capitalize	We visited france.
/	Lowercase	It is Summer.
∧	Insert	We at tacos today.
℘	Delete	I likes that movie.
⊙	Add Period	I am here
?	Add Question Mark	Who is it
!	Add Exclamation Point	Watch out
⊙	Add Comma	He lives in Ames, Iowa.
:	Add Colon	I woke up at 630.
,	Add Apostrophe	That is Bobs hat.